How do plants help us?

Bobbie Kalman

🜲 Crabtree Publishing Company

www.crabtreebooks.com

Created by Bobbie Kalman

Author and Editor-in-Chief
Bobbie Kalman

Educational consultants
Elaine Hurst
Joan King
Jennifer King

Notes for adults
Jennifer King

Editors
Kathy Middleton
Crystal Sikkens

Photo research
Bobbie Kalman

Design
Bobbie Kalman
Katherine Berti

Print and production coordinator
Katherine Berti

Prepress technician
Katherine Berti

Illustrations
Barbara Bedell: page 5
Margaret Amy Salter: page 3, 7

Photographs by Shutterstock

Library and Archives Canada Cataloguing in Publication

Kalman, Bobbie, 1947-
    How do plants help us? / Bobbie Kalman.

(My world)
Issued also in electronic format.
ISBN 978-0-7787-9561-2 (bound).--ISBN 978-0-7787-9586-5 (pbk.)

    1. Plants--Juvenile literature. I. Title. II. Series: My world
(St. Catharines, Ont.)

QK49.K326 2011   j580   C2010-907440-8

Library of Congress Cataloging-in-Publication Data

Kalman, Bobbie.
  How do plants help us? / Bobbie Kalman.
    p. cm. -- (My world)
  ISBN 978-0-7787-9586-5 (pbk. : alk. paper) -- ISBN 978-0-7787-9561-2
(reinforced library binding : alk. paper) -- ISBN 978-1-4271-9668-2
(electronic (pdf))
  1. Plants--Juvenile literature. 2. Human-plant relationships--Juvenile
literature. I. Title.
  QK49.K153 2011
  580--dc22

                                        2010047124

Crabtree Publishing Company

Printed in China/022011/RG20101116

www.crabtreebooks.com   1-800-387-7650
Copyright © **2011 CRABTREE PUBLISHING COMPANY.** All rights reserved. No part of this publication may be reproduced, stored in a retrieval system or be transmitted in any form or by any means, electronic, mechanical, photocopying, recording, or otherwise, without the prior written permission of Crabtree Publishing Company. In Canada: We acknowledge the financial support of the Government of Canada through the Canada Book Fund for our publishing activities.

Published in Canada
Crabtree Publishing
616 Welland Ave.
St. Catharines, Ontario
L2M 5V6

Published in the United States
Crabtree Publishing
PMB 59051
350 Fifth Avenue, 59th Floor
New York, New York 10118

Published in the United Kingdom
Crabtree Publishing
Maritime House
Basin Road North, Hove
BN41 1WR

Published in Australia
Crabtree Publishing
386 Mt. Alexander Rd.
Ascot Vale (Melbourne)
VIC 3032

Words to know

carbon
dioxide

forest

grains

living
thing

nectar

oxygen

photosynthesis

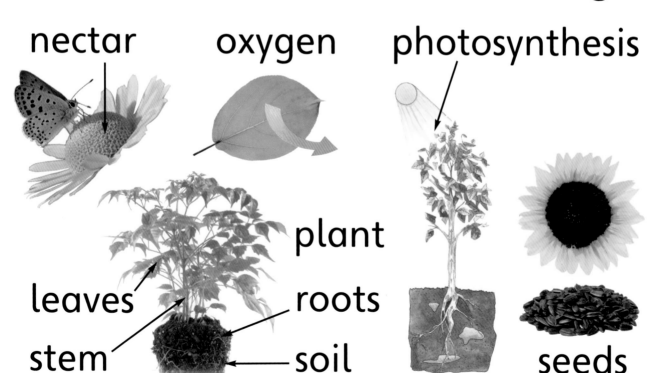

plant

leaves

roots

stem

soil

seeds

3

What is a plant?

A plant is a **living thing**.

Living things grow and change.

Living things need air, water, and sunlight.

Most plants have **leaves**, **stems**, and **roots**.

Many plants have flowers, too.

Plants can grow in **soil** or water.

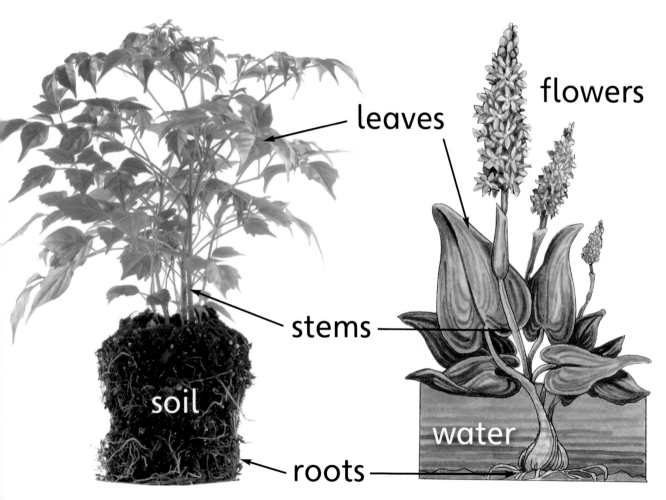

leaves

flowers

stems

soil

water

roots

Plants are the only living things that can make their own food. They use sunlight to make food from air and water.

Did you know?

Making food from sunlight is called **photosynthesis**.

Plants make food
in their leaves.
Plants give us
food to eat.

sunlight

leaves

roots

soil

water

We eat many kinds of plants. Our bread comes from plants called **grains**. Fruits and vegetables also come from plants.

Many animals also eat plants.
They eat the leaves, roots, stems,
flowers, and **seeds** of plants.
Some animals eat **nectar**.
Nectar is a sweet liquid in flowers.

seeds

When plants make food, they also make the air cleaner for us to breathe.

They change **carbon dioxide** to **oxygen**.

Too much carbon dioxide is harmful to people and animals.

Oxygen is a gas we need to breathe.

Plants use carbon dioxide to make food.

Plants give off oxygen.

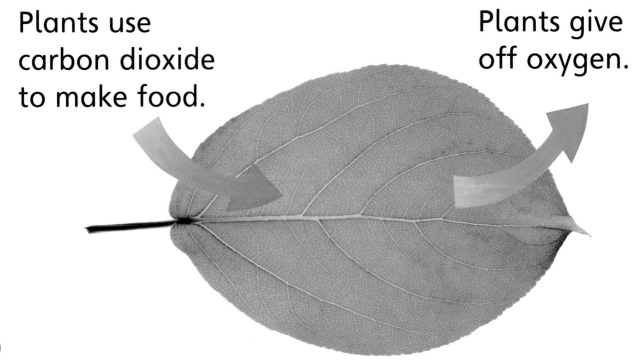

Forests are places with many trees.

They make a lot of oxygen.

They clean the air around Earth.

Trees also give us the wood
we need to build our homes.
Furniture is made from wood.
Paper is made from wood, too.

Animals also make their homes in trees.
Birds, squirrels, and monkeys live in trees.
Many animals live in the logs of trees.

baby foxes

log

You can grow plants at your home.
Planting trees will give you cleaner air.
A vegetable garden will give you fresh food.

A flower garden will bring you butterflies.

15

Notes for adults

Objectives
- to understand what plants need
- to understand how plants help people and animals
- to learn about photosynthesis

Before reading
Provide a house plant to stimulate thinking. Ask the children:
"What is this?"
"How do I take care of a plant?"
"Name three parts that most plants have." (Have the children name the leaves, stem, and roots as you point to them.)
"How do you think plants help us?"
"What questions do you have about plants?" (Make a question chart with their personal questions.)

Questions after reading the book
"What is a plant?" (living thing)
"What do plants need?" (air, water, sunlight)
"Where do plants grow?" (in soil or water)
"Where do they get their food from?" (They make it.)
"What is it called when plants make food?" (photosynthesis)

"Who needs plants?" (animals and people)
"What do plants do with carbon dioxide?" (Change it into oxygen.)
"Who needs oxygen?" (animals and people)
"How do plants help us?" (oxygen, food)
"What do forests give us?" (clean air, oxygen, wood, homes for the animals)

Activity: Writer's workshop
Ask the children to draw pictures of how plants help them and to write stories to go along with their pictures.

Extension
Provide some beans for germination. Ask each child to keep a log of his or her plant's growth from seed to plant. The children can draw pictures and/or write words. Have the children give their plants water and make sure the plants are in a place where they receive adequate sunlight.

Plants and animals in habitats
Have the children research how animals survive in nature. To learn more about baby animals in forest habitats, read Bobbie Kalman's book *Baby Animals in Forest Habitats*.

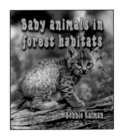

Guided reading: K

For teacher's guide, go to www.crabtreebooks.com/teachersguides